Old CUMNOCK

by
Joe Lampard

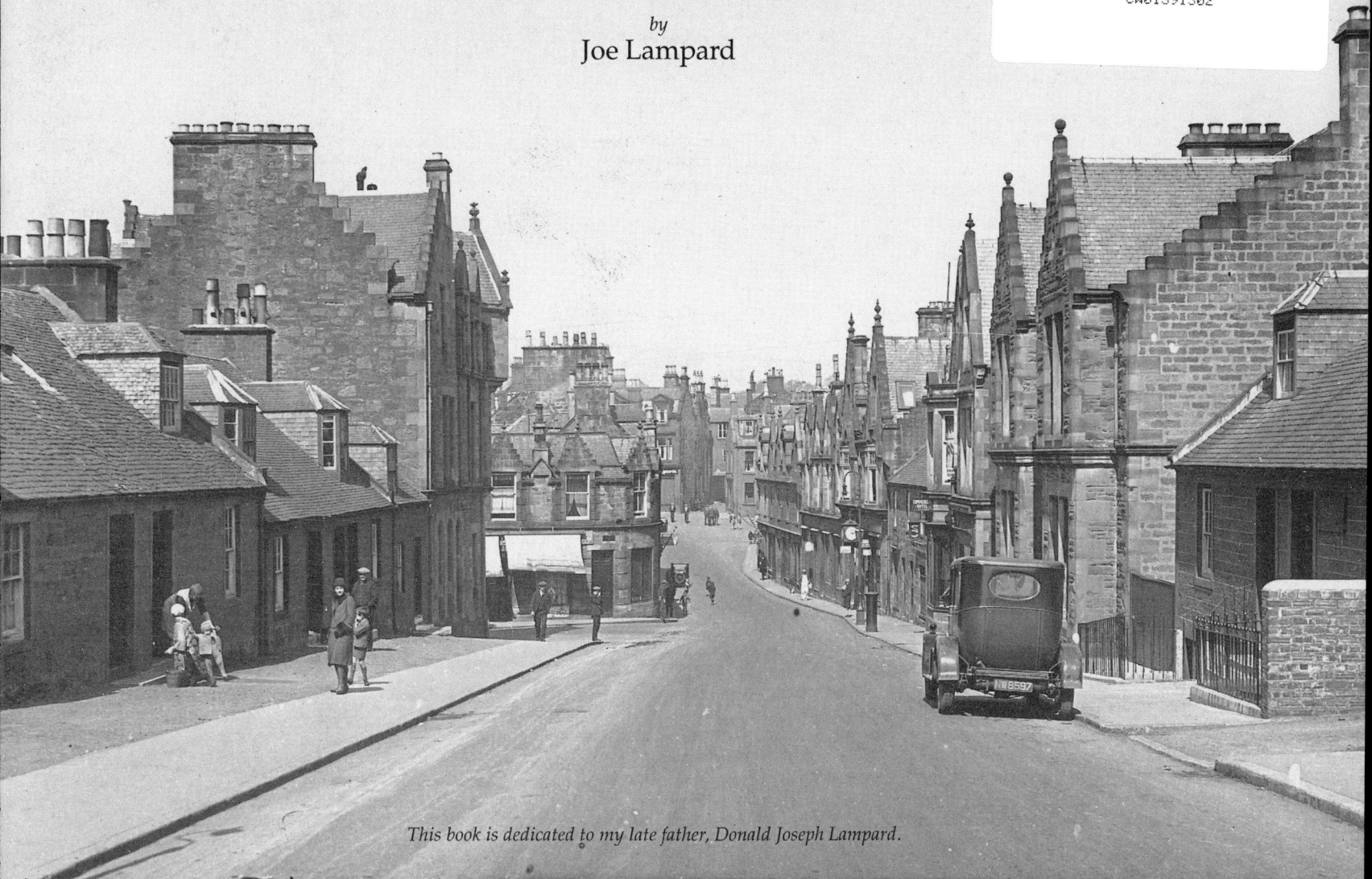

This book is dedicated to my late father, Donald Joseph Lampard.

© Joe Lampard 2005
First published in the United Kingdom, 2005,
by Stenlake Publishing Ltd.
Telephone: 01290 551122
Printed by Cordfall Ltd., Glasgow, G21 2QA

ISBN 1 84033 335 9

The publishers regret that they cannot supply copies of any pictures featured in this book.

THE WAR MEMORIAL, OLD CUMNOCK.

ACKNOWLEDGEMENTS

Many thanks to Jim Blackwood; Jim Carson; Chris Dunsmuir; Zoe Fettes; Alex, Barbara and Erine McCall; Irene McMillan (Dick Institute, Kilmarnock); Sam McVie (East Ayrshire Council Property Services); George Morton; Paul Quinn; and extra special thanks to Archie Connel and Anne Geddes of the Baird Institute in Cumnock.

FURTHER READING

The books listed below were used by the author during his research. None of them are available from Stenlake Publishing. Those interested in finding out more are advised to contact their local bookshop or reference library.

Cochrane, Drew, *The Story of Ayrshire Junior Football*, 1989
Dennison Torrie, E. P., & Coleman, Russel, *Historic Cumnock – the Scottish Burgh Survey*, Historic Scotland, 1995
Laurenson, John C. M., *Cumnock and New Cumnock in Old Picture Postcards*, European Library, 1983
Love, Dane, *Pictorial History of Cumnock*, Alloway Publishing, 1992
McIlvean, John Gardiner, *The Birth of Football in the Burns Country*
McKerrell, Thomas, & Brown, James, *Ayrshire Miners' Rows*, Ayrshire Miners Union, 1913
Moore, John, *Among Thy Green Braes*, Cumnock & Doon Valley District Council, 1977
Quail, Gerard, *The Cumnock Pottery*, Ayrshire Archaeological and Natural History Society
Steven, Helen J., *The Cumnocks Old and New*, Dunlop & Drennan, 1899
Strawhorn, John, *History of Cumnock*, Scottish Co-operative Wholesale Society
Todd, Adam Brown, *The Poetical Works of A. B. Todd*, Oliphant, Anderson & Ferrier, 1906
Cumnock & Auchinleck Ayrshire Directory, Pigot & Co., 1837
The New Statistical Account, Parish of Old Cumnock, Revd Ninian Bannatyne
The Statistical Accounts of Scotland, 1791–1799

www.cumnock.net
www.e-ayrshire.co.uk/local/clmg
www.ayrshirehistory.org.uk
www.shankly.com

Cumnock's war memorial is situated in the new cemetery in Glaisnock Street. It was unveiled in 1921 to commemorate the 117 men from the parish who perished during the First World War. A total of 662 had enlisted, sixteen of whom were decorated for outstanding service. The memorial is built of white granite and features a tall column topped with a stylised crown and a ball. The base features bronze panels listing the names of the deceased. In 1950 the memorial was extended with the addition of a five-panelled wall, allowing the names of the 37 men who gave their lives in the Second World War to be displayed.

INTRODUCTION

The earliest written reference to be found regarding Cumnock Kirk, which the town grew up around, dates from 1275 when the rectory of Cumnock paid £16 towards the Bagimond Roll (a valuation roll used as the basis for a papal tax). The kirk was built to serve Cumnock Castle (sited at New Cumnock), which in the fourteenth century was home to the Earls of March, subsequently passing to the Dunbars who held it until the seventeenth century.

In 1509 Cumnock was granted burgh of barony status by royal charter, and this date is regarded by many as marking the town's real beginning. The charter, granted by King James IV, established Cumnock as a market centre, marked by a cross, where weekly markets would take place and annual fairs were held. In 1600 the plague came to Cumnock, brought by two travelling merchants, the situation becoming so bad that at one point it was said that 'the living were hardly able to bury the dead'. The burgh changed hands about the same time, with the Earls of Dumfries taking over from the Dunbars.

The Parish of Cumnock was split into Old Cumnock and New Cumnock in 1650, and although the Earl of Dumfries had the decision annulled seventeen years later it was reimposed in 1691 and the two parishes have retained their separate identities ever since.

The next 200 years saw a slow but steady increase in Cumnock's population. By the middle of the eighteenth century there were approximately 500 residents, with most locals employed as merchants or craftsmen. The Ayrshire Turnpike Acts of 1766 and 1774 led to prodigious road-building and paved the way for much improved transport, opening up the area to new opportunities and trade. In 1787 the establishment of Catrine Cotton Works led to a marked increase in handloom weaving, and around 1800 a local man by the name of William Crawford discovered a means of manufacturing snuff boxes with an 'invisible wooden hinge'. The boxes were made from seasoned sycamore wood, decorated by painters and finished with up to 30 coats of varnish. Several of the men employed in the decoration of the boxes later found fame as celebrated artists: these included Daniel Macnee; Highland landscape artist Horatio McCulloch; and watercolourist William Leighton Leitch. The popularity of these snuff boxes spread rapidly, and by 1820 the cottage industry was employing at least 60 people in Mauchline and Auchinleck and over 100 in Cumnock. Today the snuff boxes are highly sought after collectables and regularly fetch high prices at auction. This period also saw the introduction of two new industries into the area: the manufacture of threshing machines and the opening of Cumnock Pottery, which later became well known for its 'Scotch Motto Ware'.

The arrival of the railways in the 1850s and the opening of Lugar ironworks heralded an exceptional period of growth. Coal mining started on an industrial scale at this time, with pits being opened at Stepend, Townhead, Shankston and the Barrhill, where two were located. Outside the town pits were sunk at Garlaff, Glengyron, Garrallan, Knockterra, Hindsward and Whitehill. The growth of mining brought an influx of workers from outside the area, which in turn created housing shortages. To remedy this, pit owners erected miners' rows, usually close to the pits or railway lines. By the start of the twentieth century all of the pits within the town had closed down, but production in the area still exceeded 140,000 tons of coal per year.

The first few decades of the last century saw a slow but steady decline in mining in the area, symptomatic of the general decline that was taking place in Scottish heavy industry. With the formation of the National Coal Board in 1947 a new optimism for the mining industry was born, but the board's plans to double production by the 1960s never came to fruition. The ongoing downturn in mining throughout the country was mirrored by local pit closures throughout the 60s, 70s and 80s. Today only a few opencast mines dot the local landscape.

Cumnock had become a police burgh in 1866 by the tiny margin of three votes, and became a 'small burgh' in 1929 with the passing of the Local Government Act (Scotland). The first council houses were built in the town in Urbana Terrace in 1914, followed by more in Cairn Road, Car Road and Shankston Crescent in 1920, and others in Gemmel Avenue, Gray Street, Hall Terrace and Latta Crescent in 1925. In 1954 the council proudly unveiled a plaque at 2 Holland Crescent to commemorate the building of its 1000th house. During the late 1940s Ayr County Council and St Andrew's House in Edinburgh had planned a 'new town' of 21,000 inhabitants covering Drumbrochan and Barshare, with a new town centre in the Netherthird area, but the plans never came to fruition.

1966 saw Cumnock Burgh celebrate its centenary year, with a week-long programme of music and cultural events. The town's fortunes have been mixed since then, with a continued decline in mining leading to significant losses of local jobs through the 1970s and 80s. The opening of the M77 motorway extension in 2005 has brought improved communication links with Glasgow and beyond, and the new road is likely to promote local economic growth, as well as making Cumnock increasingly popular as a commuter town. It has much to offer, with a strong industrial heritage and an attractive rural setting, and deserves to thrive again.

James Keir Hardie was born at Legbrannock in Lanarkshire on 15 August 1856, the illegitimate son of a miner. Some years later his mother Mary Keir married a ship's carpenter. His formative years were spent in extreme poverty and James started his working life as a baker's delivery boy at the tender age of eight. By the time he was ten he had started working in the Lanarkshire coal mines, and despite the twelve-hour shifts he still managed to make time for reading and writing lessons with his mother. In 1880, the year of his marriage to Lillias Balfour Wilson of Hamilton, he helped establish a union at his colliery, leading to the first organised strike of Lanarkshire miners. This resulted in his dismissal and prompted his move to the town of Old Cumnock. A year later James Keir Hardie became secretary of the newly formed Ayrshire Miners' Association, leading his members on a ten-week strike for both better wages and working conditions. He also started work as a journalist for the *Cumnock News*, writing a weekly column entitled 'Black Diamonds' under the pen-name 'The Trapper', and eventually becoming the newspaper's editor. In 1886 he was employed as secretary of the Scottish Miners' Federation and a year later started publishing his own monthly journal, *The Miner*, which later became the *Labour Leader*. On 26 August 1888 James Keir Hardie became a founding member and chairman of the Scottish Labour Party and in the 1892 general election he stood as the Independent Labour candidate for West Ham South in London's industrial East End, his victory making him the country's first socialist MP. Keir Hardie also held the chairmanship of the Independent Labour Party between 1893 and 1900, and again between 1913 and 1915. In 1900 he was elected MP for Merthyr Tydfil in Wales and held this position until his death on 6 September 1915.

Lochnorris was built for James Keir Hardie in 1891 on Auchinleck Road at a cost of £600, paid for with an interest-free loan from long-time supporter Adam Birkmyre. Many of the politician's speeches and writings were penned in the summerhouse at the bottom of the garden, overlooking the Lugar Water. After Keir Hardie's death in 1915, Lochnorris remained the family home. His widow Lillias died nine years later in 1924, the year of their daughter Nan's wedding to Emrys Hughes, after which Nan and Emrys continued to live in Lochnorris. Both became active in local politics. Emrys was Provost of Cumnock from 1934–35, later becoming MP for South Ayrshire, while his wife succeeded him as provost in 1935 and held the position until her death in July 1947. Emrys Hughes remarried in 1949, and his second wife, Martha Cleland, bequeathed the 'Lochnorris Collection' to the local council in 1982. Some items from the collection are now on display in the Baird Institute.

Opposite: This photograph illustrates the hustle and bustle of the Square during a fair day in 1881. Fairs had originally been held near Stepend's Ford, but due to the proximity of the tanning works in the Tanyard and the building of Stepend's Bridge in the middle of the eighteenth century the fair was moved to the mercat cross in Townhead Street and then to the Square. The main business of fair days was the selling of farm produce, though entertainers were also in attendance and there were stalls run by local shops and merchants. Fair days were also used by farmers to engage workers from the town, with the May fair and the Scythe fair (July) being the busiest, in preparation for the forthcoming harvests. The March fair day was a town favourite, no doubt because of the horse race which took place with up to a dozen entrants. The first races were run along Ayr Road to Burnside and back, and the event was later moved to a field owned by the Dumfries Arms Hotel.

CUMNOCKS WELCOME HOME TO LORD & LADY BUTE. III.

The return to Cumnock in September 1905 of John Crichton Stuart and Augusta Mary Monica Bellingham – Lord and Lady Bute – following their marriage in June at Kilsaran in Ireland. The couple were met by an entourage of over 70 horsemen and local dignitaries in carriages at Cumnock Station, which had been decorated by the stationmaster, as described by the *Chronicle* of 15 September: 'flags floated from all points of vantage, and the Marquess and Marchioness had to pass through no fewer than three arches composed of oak branches relieved with sprays of flowers'. From there they were taken by carriage through the crowded streets down Barrhill Road, along Hamilton Place, round the Square, down Glaisnock Street into Ayr Road and finally back to Dumfries Estate. As a wedding gift the people of Cumnock gave Lady Bute a 'very beautiful diamond and ruby bracelet the cost of which is well over £300' (ibid.). Parades like this attracting large crowds were fairly regular occurrences at one time, with the Butes celebrating comings of age and birthdays as well as weddings in the town.

This picture of the Square probably dates from the first decade of the twentieth century and shows the mercat cross topped by a gas lamp. Tower Street runs behind the row of shops on the right, deriving its name from the Blue Tower Inn which was built in 1666 and was the principal hostelry in the town for many years. The Royal Hotel, facing the camera, was at one point home to Cumnock's 'Winsome Willie Club', a Burns' club. The current building was erected around 1892 by R. J. Barrowman and the hotel was taken over by Stevenson's Dairy Farms in 1956, which opened a bakery shop in the old tearooms in 1964. Today the hotel is owned by local businessman Robert Kyle. From about 1800 handball was a popular pastime among local children and for many years was played in the Square against the walls and shuttered windows of the kirk. Businesses along the right-hand side of the Square included J. A. Bingham, fishmonger; James McGrady, boot and shoemaker; and R. B. Houston, jeweller.

The Lugar Water with the 'Box Church' on the left and the spire of the Crichton Memorial Church, on Ayr Road, beyond it. The Cumnock Associate Church, or Box Church, was built in 1831 at a cost of £876.11s. and replaced an earlier church dating from 1775. It is the oldest surviving church building in Cumnock and recently opened as a cafe after lying empty for many years. The land on which the church was built was purchased from John Murdoch, and at the time of its construction the Earl of Dumfries's factor refused to sell the builders any sand. Soon afterwards both the Lugar and Glaisnock Waters flooded, bringing a fresh supply of sand from upstream in what the parishioners believed to be a miracle (the church sits beside the Glaisnock Water near where it joins the Lugar Water). The Tanyard, adjacent to the church, derives its name from the fact that this riverside location was once the site of a tanning works, situated near the join of the rivers in which the noxious waste associated with the leather-making process would have been dumped. In 1793 the tanner working from these premises supplied leather to over 60 shoemakers. With government backing and the purchase of a proper motor fire engine, the Tanyard became the site of Cumnock's fire station in 1940. A new bus station opened there in June 1966 allowing the Square to be pedestrianised.

Lugar Street, Cumnock.

John Baird was born in Lugar Street in 1813, where his father David kept the Tup Inn after tenanting the farm at Longmore on Logan Estate for many years. John was an only son and upon leaving school was sent to learn joinery. During this period he also read extensively, particularly enjoying science and art. At a young age he developed an aptitude for drawing, which continued as a young man, and he would regularly walk the few miles to Catrine to be instructed by one of the draughtsman from the cotton mill there. When his father died, John Baird inherited a considerable amount of property in Lugar Street, some of which he demolished in the 1860s, making way for a building that he later ran as a drapery store.

When John Baird died on 27 July 1888, aged 75, he left his estate to provide a public building on his land in Cumnock containing a museum, recreation and reading rooms. Mrs Brakenridge, wife of the then town clerk, opened the Baird Institute three years later on 2 March 1891. It was designed by a Mr Ingram of Kilmarnock, the son of Baird's early instructor in drawing at Catrine Mill, in Scottish Baronial style, and was built from pink sandstone quarried locally at Auchinleck. Gas lighting originally illuminated all the rooms, each of which contained an Irish white marble fireplace, with the exception of the billiards room which featured a magnificent Italian black and gold marble fireplace. Trustees administered the Baird Institute until 1972, when it was transferred to the ownership of Cumnock Burgh which undertook major refurbishment work. An annual acquisition fund was also established, enabling artefacts of local historical significance to be purchased and put on public display. Today the Baird Institute contains a wide range of resources which relate to the history of the local area including archives, family history material, books, maps, microfilms, museum collections, newspapers and photographs. John Baird's main personal studies were of mechanical drawing, with examples of this work on display today in the collection.

Lugar Street looking towards the Square. The Tup Inn, in the centre of the picture, was formerly run by John Baird's father. It has now been demolished, as have the two-storey dwelling-house and thatched cottage on the right which disappeared in 1966 when the Tanyard was widened. The corner of Lugar Street and the Square, beside Bank Lane, was the site of Cumnock's first school. In 1804 a new parish school replaced it on the site in the Square now occupied by the Clydesdale Bank. For a while Lugar Street was home to Cumnock's Municipal Bank, which was established on 2 April 1928, giving all its profits to the town council.

Stepend's Pit, where coal was mined from under the Glebe on the Cumnock side of the Lugar Water from 1853 to 1892, was the source of Stepend's Bing, the location for this early panoramic view of Cumnock. The Congregational Church, sitting just behind the ornate gardens to the left, was built at a cost of £2,100 in 1882, in what was then still part of Auchinleck Parish. For a short time it was the church attended by Keir Hardie. The field to the right of the picture is the Holm, known locally in the late nineteenth century as 'Boo't [Bowed] Scotland'. It was part of Woodend Farm and used to be where travelling circuses set up their attractions before later moving to an area within the nearby Woodroad Park. Only a few houses in Auchinleck Road had been built when the picture was taken, including Holmhead, Broomfield and the United Presbyterian Church manse, the spaces being filled in during a major housing development which took place in the early 1950s.

Another view from Stepend's Bing, this time looking towards the Glebe with Wood Road on the left. The building in the foreground was at one point owned by an Alexander Duncan and known as Sandbed Mill. In 1692 Mr Duncan sold the business to George McGawn, but retained ownership of the lands of Barshare and Waterside. Sandbed later became King's Mill and traded as Speir's bakery for many years before eventually being destroyed by fire in 1963. In the early 1950s the Glebe was purchased by the burgh and a scheme of 60 houses built on it, with the streets – Robertson Avenue, Warrick Drive and McDonald Street – named after former local miners. This was a busy period of development, with houses also being built in Hearth Road, Elizabeth Crescent, Coila Place and the Holm, plus a further 200 houses in Drumbrochan, all within four years of each other. In the distance is Bank Viaduct, which crosses the Lugar Water and was officially opened on 20 May 1850. It was built by John Miller of Miller & Grainger, the Edinburgh contractors who had built Ballochmyle Viaduct a few years earlier. The highest of the viaduct's thirteen arches stands at 175 feet.

Glaisnock Street looking down the Brae towards the area (on the right) originally known as Greenbraehead or Potters Row. Cumnock Pottery was started in 1792, mainly to produce graphite crucibles for the 6th Earl of Dumfries who wanted to develop a blast furnace complex to better exploit the ironstone and coal deposits on his estates. James Taylor, famed as being a pioneer of steam navigation, managed the pottery for many years and after his death on 18 September 1825 control passed to his son Robert. For many years it was run at a loss, and it wasn't until 1857, when James McGavin Nicol took over, that the business realised its full potential and became known throughout the country. The pottery's change in fortune was due to the 'Motto Ware' which it started producing around this time. In its heyday it manufactured jam pots, sugar bowls, milk jugs, salt crocks, teapots, candlesticks and many more items, which were mainly finished with a brown and cream glaze and adorned with various mottoes. The pottery eventually closed in 1920, citing 'a shortage of easily dug clay and a fashion change towards imported china'.

Peden Mont, Old Cumnock

Barrhill Road was the original site of Cumnock's gallows, and eventually became the location of the town's graveyard. Peden's Monument is the best-known tomb in the graveyard, but close to this can be found the lesser-known resting place of Thomas Richard, an 80-year-old tenant farmer from Muirkirk who was executed in Cumnock Square as a covenanter on 5 April 1685. After his execution he was buried on Gallows Knowe, becoming the first covenanter to be laid to rest at this spot. His crime had been to give food and shelter to a group of fugitive covenanters. Just behind Richard's stone is the burial place of David Dun and Simon Paterson, also executed as covenanters in 1685. The site is marked by an old, weather-worn stone which has recently been supplemented with a new stone commissioned by the Scottish Covenanter Memorials Association. Also in the graveyard is the stone of William Simson, immortalised by Robert Burns as 'Winsome Willie'. The stone is inscribed with a poem by Adam Brown Todd.

Peden's Monument was erected in 1891 and dedicated on Thursday 16 July 1892 in front of a crowd of between three and four thousand onlookers. The memorial, marking the final resting place of the Revd Alexander Peden, the 'prophet of the covenant', is made of Aberdeen granite and was designed by R. S. Ingram. The inscription 'Buried here out of contempt' refers to the story of the desecration of Peden's original grave in Auchinleck Parish. Dragoons exhumed his body, planning to hang his corpse on a gibbet in Old Cumnock, but the townspeople and Lady Dumfries intervened and prevented them from doing so. Instead, as a final insult to Peden, the troops interred his body in the shadow of the gallows.

The Crichton family built Hillside House, originally known as Hillside Cottage, near the foot of Barrhill Road in 1846. It was a beautiful villa whose garden was 'kept in the most exquisite order' with 'its flower-beds . . . bright with all the colours of the rainbow' (John Strawhorn, *History of Cumnock*). The gardens also housed a conservatory, vinery and greenhouse in which 'every kind of fruit and flower in their season [could] be found' (ibid.).

In 1909 the house came on the market at £1,500, and Cumnock School Board borrowed £3,500 from the Public Works Loans Board to purchase it and convert it to a school. Hillside House was opened as the Higher Grade School in 1911, with an initial intake of 143 pupils who had previously been schooled across the road at the old parish schoolroom. This picture illustrates the alterations that were made to the building.

This photograph, taken in 1930 after Hillside House had been demolished but before an additional east wing was added in 1939, shows what was originally an extension to the Higher Grade School. This opened on 31 October 1926 and became the main school building after Hillside House was demolished. In 1927 the school was renamed Cumnock Academy. Prior to the building of the extension, some lessons had been taught in army huts, erected in the grounds to help relieve classroom overcrowding. The new building comprised a dozen classrooms, staff rooms, science labs and a gymnasium with a small swimming pool. On its opening Cumnock Academy had a roll of 900 pupils, but by 1948 it had grown to become the largest school in Ayrshire with 1,443 pupils. In the late 1960s, with the construction of the new Cumnock Academy in Ayr Road, the building became a primary school and is presently known as Greenmill Primary School.

Left: Janet Livingstone founded Livingstone's grocery store on Lugar Street in 1861, initially trading from a thatched cottage further down the street before moving into these premises at No. 15 around 1880. The general grocer's was later managed by her son Robert, who served as chairman of the parish council between 1910 and 1919. Robert's son James then ran the shop for 50 years until 1967. After James's retiral it continued to trade under the name Livingstone's until its eventual closure in 1982. This picture shows David Connell and senior assistant David Hannah outside the shop. The initials VR on the window indicate that it was taken before 1901, during the reign of Queen Victoria.

This later view of Livingstone's shows the shop after John Baird's adjoining premises had been purchased to allow it to be extended. Robert Livingstone was a familiar sight around Cumnock with his horse and carriage, which he used to deliver goods to the outlying areas and country estates. Pictured here, from left to right, are Alex Lindsay; David Connell, who worked for three generations of the family over a period of 59 years; Mrs Kay; Robert Livingstone, the then manager; and David McCulley.

Alexander Muir of Paisley opened what was considered to be Cumnock's 'first practical grocer' at 9 Townhead Street in 1859. After his death in 1886, the grocery and wine merchant's business passed to his son James and was run by successive members of the family until it finally shut its doors in 1964. Muir's was well-known locally for its 'Corsegellioch' whisky, named after the hill to the south of Cumnock. The whisky, which was bottled on Muir's premises, was a fine blend that included peaty Ardbeg malt from Islay and Cambus whisky from Clackmannanshire. Alexander Muir was one of the nine signatories of the petition which led to the establishment of Cumnock Burgh in 1866.

This picture shows Charlie Merry and the staff of Black Bull Taxis, the first taxi service to operate in Cumnock. The business operated from the Black Bull Garage for many years, situated just off the Square behind what is now the Mercat Hotel, formerly the Black Bull Hotel. This was an important part of Cumnock life for many years, with its halls being used for meetings by various groups, both religious and secular. Black Bull Close was also the site at one point of McGavin's bakery, a family-run bakery that made the famous Cumnock Tarts and was something of an institution in the town.

John Ballantine's photographic studio was situated on the bend of Ayr Road. John and his brother Duncan, who owned and ran a newsagent's and printer's business on Glaisnock Street, served as town commissioners with the local council for a number of years. Duncan went on to be editor of the *Cumnock Chronicle* and John was one of the original trustees of the Baird Institute, donating a collection of stuffed animals as well as some excellent examples of his photographic work. These can still be seen in the Baird, along with a portrait of the man with his beloved box camera.

McCartney's engineering firm was established at Clockclownie Farm, just south of the town, in 1812, moving to Burnside in Cumnock in 1832. The company was best known for its threshing machines (some constituent parts of which can be seen in the foreground), mill equipment and bridge frameworks, a good example being Rifleman's Bridge over the Lugar Water, which was moved to Greenholm in the 1920s and finally taken down a decade later. On 6 June 1842 Kirkpatrick MacMillan gave his first public demonstration of the pedal-powered bicycle in Cumnock, allowing McCartney's to copy the cumbersome machine during his stay. Following George McCartney's death in 1868 at the age of 78, the company continued to trade under his name until 1901 when it was taken over by Charles and Andrew Taylor, who specialised in electrical switchgear for mining and shipbuilding. The company was eventually wound up in 1933, 21 years after celebrating its centenary. Pictured here, left to right, are:
Back row: Andrew Taylor, George Milne, J. Corbett, Bill Simpson, H. Dalziel, J. Marshall
Front row: Johnny Pyle, Archibald Miller, Harry Kennedy, ____ Hodge, Jim Duncan, Owen Finn, J. Cooper

Cumnock's original curling pond was situated at Townhead, and in 1886 the curling club and burgh council agreed to enlarge and repair it, after which it was also used as a reservoir to 'flush' the Glaisnock Water. Woodhead curling pond on the Dumfries Estate was also in use at this time, and although considered a superior rink was less convenient for the townspeople, as described by the *Cumnock Chronicle* of 2 June 1905: 'Formerly it occupied a whole day to go to Woodhead, play a game, and get home again'. In 1905 Lord Bute donated a field off the Ayr Road to the club where a large pond was dug out, although this was eventually abandoned due to its inability to hold water effectively. No doubt members of the club would have been good customers of Kay's of Scotland, the famous curling stone manufacturer based in Mauchline.

Opposite: A football team was formed in Cumnock in 1875, playing at New Station Park, now part of the new cemetery. The team's colours were maroon shirts and white shorts, and in the 1884–85 cup final they beat Mauchline 3–2. A new club called Springbank appeared in 1894, but by the turn of the century they were no longer among the seniors, continuing for a time as Cumnock Thistle and then Cumnock Celtic. In 1912 a group of local, football-minded men were at work, including William McMillan, Joe Bairn and Tom Burns, and they joined with others to form Cumnock Juniors. The Juniors' first match was a 3–3 draw, played at New Station Park in August 1913. They joined the Western League in 1934, becoming champions in 1935–36 on what was the first of several occasions. In 1915/16, 1917/18 and 1948/49 they won the famous Challenge Cup, and over the years have won many other trophies including the Ayrshire Cup, the Vernon Trophy, the Western League and Cup, the Ayrshire League Cup and the Ayrshire District Cup. The Juniors' finest hour came on 19 May 1979 at Hampden Park, when they beat Bo'ness United 1–0 to win the Scottish Junior Cup for the first time in their history, repeating this feat ten years later with a 1–0 win against Ormiston Primrose at Rugby Park, Kilmarnock in 1989. This Cumnock Juniors line-up is thought to date from the 1920s and includes goalkeeper William 'Bones' McCall (so-called because he was so thin and wore two or three jerseys to make himself look bigger), club officials Andrew 'Dusky' MacCall (middle row, far right), Jock McHarlan (middle row, far left), 'Tinker' McMurdo, Harry 'Buff' Kennedy and Willie McGregor.

For many years the people of Cumnock had wanted some sort of public park, and although their hopes were raised in 1897 proposals for a Jubilee Park came to nothing. In 1907 the Marquess of Bute handed the care and running of the Townhead Park to the burgh – an area that had long been used for football, curling and other sports – but no further facilities were provided. Ten years later, following the bequest of the estate of the Misses Murray, formerly of the Dumfries Arms Hotel, the Murray Trust was established with the intention of creating a public park within the town. For legal reasons long delays ensued, although finally, a full twelve years after the trust was set up, the ten-acre Murray Park was opened with swings, playing fields and seating. Taken in 1930, this photograph shows the 'witches hat', a later addition to the park and a favourite of children at the time.

This picture shows the large paddling pool which was once one of the many leisure facilities in Woodroad Park. In 1937 25 acres of land were purchased at Wood Road for £500, with the swimming pool provided at a cost of £5,500 and a total of around £9,000 spent by 1939. That year plans were drawn up for a gymnasium, but the war forced the abandonment of this and other schemes. Despite this there were three tennis courts, a putting green, cafe, pavilion, football, rugby and cricket pitches, with an asphalt, open-air dance floor added after the war, followed in 1951 by a children's play park. Woodroad Park proved an attraction to people from outside the town and was an ideal spot for Sunday school trips, scout rallies and camps. West of Scotland cyclists have regularly held their annual rallies here, and at one time it was a popular camping and caravanning site.

BATHING POOL CUMNOCK

Local miners dug out the swimming pool (measuring 100 feet by 45 feet and increasing in depth from three to ten feet) by hand, the earth being removed by horse and cart. Shortly after opening, several local swimming clubs were formed and each summer the local authority provided swimming lessons for pupils from the town and surrounding area. Regular swimming galas attracted large crowds and the pool was also host to Scottish swimming and diving championships, exhibition displays and international swimming and water polo contests.

Opposite: When Provost Nan Hardie Hughes, daughter of James Keir Hardie, opened Cumnock swimming pool in June 1936 it was one of the earliest and best outdoor pools in the country. Crowds of over 2,500 gathered for the occasion and were entertained by 'aquatic celebrities' of the time, including David Crabb, the former Scottish diving champion, and Ellen King, who had represented Great Britain at the Olympics and was the only swimmer to have held Scottish records for every style and distance.

Lady Bute's Hospital, or Bute Hospital, was gifted to the people of Cumnock in 1882. The small cottage hospital was staffed by trained nurses of the Sisters of the Sacred Heart and comprised ten beds and three cots. It was used for all types of medical cases and often treated the victims of local mining accidents. Four years after its opening Lord and Lady Bute built St John's School in Bank Avenue, adjacent to the Bute Hospital. Following the establishment of the National Health Service in 1948, the wartime hospital at Ballochmyle was extended and became the main hospital for the area. Bute Hospital was closed down and the local committee which had maintained it since 1920 was disbanded. The building has since been demolished, with the site now occupied by Murray Court. Ballochmyle Hospital itself has now also closed and been demolished, following the opening of a new community hospital on Ayr Road in 2000.

In 1893 the county council put forward proposals for a hospital on Barrhill Road on a plot adjacent to the local slaughterhouse. The choice of site met with much dissension and argument from the townspeople and town council, as Sandy Barrowman wrote: 'What's this the county council want? What gumption they disclose, man! A fever hospital they'll plant, beneath our very nose, man!' (A. B. Todd, *The Poetical Works of A. B. Todd*). Eventually, in 1898, with approval from the Marquess of Bute, the townspeople managed to persuade the council to locate the hospital on the outskirts of the town. Holmhead Hospital for Infectious Diseases was thus opened and served Cumnock for many years, with patients being taken by ambulance to the hospital wrapped in a red blanket. With a decline in the incidence of infectious diseases and tuberculosis, Holmhead Hospital, like the nearby Glenafton Sanatorium, was converted into a nursing home for the chronically sick and aged.

Cumnock's town hall was built by public subscription on a site donated by the Marquess of Bute, with work commencing in 1883 and the building completed and opened on 7 June 1885. As well as fulfilling a civic function, it has been a popular venue for weekend dances and concerts since its establishment, and over the years has been used for a wide variety of purposes. In the 1930s it served as a junior instruction centre for unemployed juveniles; during the Second World War it was used by military units stationed in the town; and in 1947 it accommodated classes from Cumnock Academy because of a shortage of space at the school. In 1930 the hall played host to midget golf, in 1936 roller-skating was on offer, and from 1957 it was used for bingo, which drew such crowds that a town council meeting of December 1959 was disturbed. The town hall was also a popular concert venue throughout the late 60s and early 70s, with bands such as Status Quo, The Who and Slade all playing there. A bronze bust of Keir Hardie stands outside the building on Glaisnock Street, the work of Benno Schotz RSA. It was gifted to the town by the Keir Hardie Memorial Committee in August 1939.

Prior to the Cumnock Picture House opening in 1913, the town hall held occasional nights of 'cinematographic entertainment' which proved popular with locals but something of a headache for staff. Great care had to be taken when moving the four-ton portable engine and dynamo (used to generate the power required to screen the films) in and out of the venue! For a number of years cinematograph shows had also been offered at fairs in the Square. No doubt inspired by the popularity of these screenings, plans were put in place for a dedicated cinema and the Cumnock Picture House opened its doors for business on 31 March. The inaugural film, shown to a packed house, was *The Count of Monte Cristo*. Films were screened nightly, with two shows on a Monday and Saturday and a Saturday matinee for children. As well as serving as a cinema, the occasional Vaudeville night was also held until the building became a bingo hall. It continues as a popular venue for bingo to this day. This picture shows it before a more decorative facade (visible on the facing page) was added.

Hamilton Place nestles between Cumnock Square and the Barrhill. In 1903 the original thatched cottages were replaced by an elegant row of shops which upon opening were occupied by, from left to right: John Goldie, draper; John Andrew, chemist; Grace Samson, draper; Thomas McGauchie, barber; and Hugh Black, solicitor. All of the shops, except Goldie's, were later bought by the Auchinleck Co-operative Society and established as its main shop in Cumnock, replacing the premises which had been opened on Glaisnock Street in January 1934. In April 1956 the co-op modernised the shops, adding a second floor and sadly removing the ornate wooden frontages. Goldie's old premises housed a television rental shop for a while and is today occupied by a beautician's.

Townhead Street, the original site of the cross, would once have been home to Cumnock's bustling market place and busy fair days. A new mercat cross was erected in 1703, then moved in 1769 close to its current location in the Square. The low thatched cottages in this picture were originally home to Cumnock's weaving community. Weaving expanded steadily from the eighteenth century, enjoying its heyday in the 1820s when upwards of 120 looms were in production. Its demise in the 1860s was brought about by a decline in trade mainly due to the Civil War in America and the introduction of the power loom. By the end of the century only three weavers remained in business. In the 1880s Townhead Street also became home to the Townhead Smithy, opened by Henry Merry from Maybole. The property then became Mill's ironmonger's before its current incarnation as Timbermills.

The building on the corner of Glaisnock Street and Ayr Road, which at one time was home to Mary Miller's confectionery shop, was the original site of Cumnock's toll cottage. This was later replaced by two tollgates: one further along Ayr Road at Bridgend and another at Pottery Row on Glaisnock Street. When this postcard was produced in the early years of the twentieth century the shops on the right-hand side of the picture were occupied by Robert Brown, weaver and tweed seller, and R. & A. Allan, watchmaker. These premises had at one time been owned by Turnbull & Allan, watchmakers. For many years the clock outside the shop was a favourite meeting place for townspeople: an anonymous local gifted it to Cumnock in 1918 and in 1920 it was repaired and lit. The clock was struck and knocked down by a double-decker bus in July 1963 and in 1965 was replaced by a new one on the adjacent co-op building. In *Notes on the Way Through Ayrshire*, written over 100 years ago, Glaisnock Street is described as 'the best street in the town . . . lined on both sides with first-class shops, and [containing] the publishing offices of two weekly newspapers'.

This view, looking up Glaisnock Street from Townhead, shows the incline that has variously been known as Munn's Brae, McKinlay's Brae and Heid Inn's Brae. The latter name referred to the New Inn, or Heid Inn, which opened in March 1717 and played an important part in Cumnock's history as a popular coaching inn. In 1840 it became the Dumfries Arms, and in 1887 the newly formed Cumnock Burns Club started holding its annual meetings there. Famous visitors to the inn included Sir Walter Scott and Robert Burns. Further up the brae is St Andrew's United Free Church, designed by Donald McDonald, which opened its doors on 3 June 1939. Also located on the brae is 'Windyhills', the former home of renowned journalist, author and poet Adam Brown Todd. This was built with the assistance of a Mr John Hyslop, the laird of Bank and Afton, after Todd had saved the lives of both him and his son following a carriage crash.

Ayr Road was laid out in the late eighteenth century and became one of the main thoroughfares in and out of the town. Tenants of the shops seen here included Hugh Lorimer, clothier; Millar's millinery; and Mary Miller's confectionery shop (just visible on the right). Her premises were taken over prior to the First World War by Mario Luni as the Welcome Cafe, which became something of a Cumnock institution. The Lunis' ice cream, freshly made on the premises, was famous throughout the area. Ernesto Luni took over after Mario's retiral and remained in business until the building was demolished. On the opposite corner from the cafe is the imposing Bank of Scotland building, designed by Peddie & Kinnear of Kilmarnock and built in 1870. Prior to this the Cumnock branch of the Bank of Scotland had been operated as a joint venture between Matthew MacKerrow and Hamilton Rose from MacKerrow's home (he was a local cloth merchant). When the bank moved to its present premises in Townhead Street the building on Ayr Road became a printer's and then a solicitor's office, which it remains today.

Cumnock from Shankstone Bing

This view from Shankston Bing shows the twin greens of Cumnock Bowling Club. Formed in 1868, the club opened with one green and added a second one in 1882. It has enjoyed a number of successes over the years, winning the Scottish Rink Championship in 1937 and the Scottish Pairs Championship two years later. Robert Cowan, one of the club's most successful members, won numerous trophies before going on to become a prominent figure within the Scottish Bowling Association. In 1958 he was nominated to the International Bowling Board. The 140-foot spire in the background belongs to Cumnock's Crichton Memorial Church on Ayr Road. Built between 1896 and 1899, the church was gifted to the community by Miss Crichton of Hillside in memory of her father, Hew Crichton, and brother Sheriff James Arthur Crichton, both of whom died within a few days of each other in 1892. The Revd John Warrick was the first minister in charge, serving the Free Church from 1883 until his death in 1931. During his lifetime he did much for the local community, and in 1899 wrote *The History Of Old Cumnock*.

Opposite: This view of Cumnock town centre shows preparations underway in 1973–74 for the building of the Glaisnock Shopping Centre. Constructed on the site of old premises in Waterside Place and Townhead Street, there was strong opposition from many residents about the proposed development, but it went ahead regardless. The white building on the right of the picture now operates as a taxi office and just behind it the Craighead Inn can be seen. The building it occupies dates from the early 1700s, with this part of town, including Craighead Close, regarded as containing some of the oldest surviving buildings in Cumnock. From 1915 the local fire brigade stored equipment at the inn, and it is reputed that the attic of the building is haunted.

Bridge at Dumfries House, Cumnock.

RELIABLE WR&S SERIES.

The elegant three-arch Avenue Bridge, or Adam Bridge as it is commonly known, is notable for being the only river-crossing designed by the Adam family. It stands within the grounds of Dumfries Estate, which also includes two single-arch bridges, an icehouse, a coach house, lodges, a temple, the ruins of Terringzean Castle and a dovecote erected in 1671 and restored in 1842. In the nineteenth century the Marquess of Bute's Dumfries Estate covered the greater part of Old Cumnock and its adjoining parishes, amounting in 1872 to a total of 43,734 acres. With the workings of the estate, its mineral rights and other concerns it was said that 'so wealthy were the coal-mining Butes in the nineteenth century that they were said to account for a third of Britain's gross national product' (Magnus Linklater, *Scotsman*).

Leifnoreis was a strong, stone tower erected in the fourteenth century by the Craufuirds, who held the surrounding land (part of which became the Dumfries Estate) until the mid-seventeenth century. It was the 5th Earl of Dumfries, William, who commissioned the Adam brothers to build Dumfries House near the site of the old tower, following his succession to the title in 1742. The foundation stone was laid on 18 July 1754 and building work was completed five years later in 1759. Dumfries House was the first important country commission for the brothers following the death of their father, William Adam, who had initially been asked to design the mansion. To their credit the cost of the project was kept to within a few pence of the original estimate of £7,979.11s.2d. The wings of the house were never completed to the Adams' original design, but were finished in 1905 by Robert Weir Schultz for the then Marquess of Bute. Dumfries House contains Chippendale furniture which has remained intact and in situ ever since it was bought by Lord Dumfries straight out of Thomas Chippendale's workshop in London in 1759. The house has 'the largest and most representative collection of eighteenth century Scottish furniture known to exist anywhere' (David Jones, St Andrews University), including furniture from Edinburgh craftsmen Alexander Peter and William Mathie.

Glaisnock House was designed and built by James Ingram of Kilmarnock around 1833 for James Allason, the Glaisnock Estate having been purchased by Alexander Allason in 1797. During the 1850s ownership of the estate passed from the Allasons to Captain Robert Campbell, who was originally from Auchmannoch in Sorn Parish. Glaisnock Estate was broken up just over 50 years later, with the elegant mansion, which had by then been extended, being bought by the county council. It was subsequently opened as a junior secondary school in 1952, specialising mainly in rural education and taking both day pupils and boarders. Glaisnock was upgraded to a 'four-year school' in 1968, but was closed in June 1973. It later reopened as a residential centre for outdoor studies, but this closed in 1996. The house was sold by the local authority on 29 July 2002 and is currently undergoing major refurbishment before opening in the near future as an outreach education centre.

Garrallan House and Estate have a long and varied history, with the Campbell family, who owned much land in the Parish of Cumnock in the fourteenth century, in possession of them for several centuries. They passed to the Douglas family when Margaret Campbell married George Douglas, and were inherited by their eldest son, Hugh, in 1676. The most notable member of the family was Dr Patrick Douglas, one of Robert Burns's associates, who suffered crippling financial losses in the Ayr Bank crash of 1772. Until 1792 the Douglases were paid an annual premium for not working their coal deposits at Garrallan, but thereafter leased the mineral rights, forcing down the price of coal from nearby Garlaff pit. The house and estate were again passed on via marriage when Jane Douglas married Hamilton Boswell of Knockroon, and remained within the Boswell family until sold in 1914 to the Stevensons of Changue. Notable features on the building include five date stones – 1660, 1676, 1856, 1868 and 1874 – believed to mark both new additions to the building and significant points in the history of its owners. Garrallan House is currently undergoing major redevelopment.

LOGAN HS. OLD CUMNOCK

At one point Logan House Estate comprised 3,700 acres, but like many local estates it was broken up in the 1920s. The elegant country mansion was built in the early nineteenth century by William Allason, the land having been purchased in 1800 from a Mr Hamilton, a wealthy Glasgow merchant. Hamilton had bought the estate from its most famous occupant, Hugh Logan, better known as the 'Laird of Logan'. There was said to be a stone on the estate, known as Logan's Pillar, where its namesake would while away many an hour in conversation, cracking jokes and imparting witticisms to those around him. Not all members of the parish appreciated Logan's sarcasm and wit though, and the Revd Ninian Bannatyne once said of his utterances that 'from the frequent mixture of coarseness and profanity that interlard them, they have by no means contributed to promote the interests, either of religion or morality, in the neighbourhood'. Logan House was later demolished and is today the site of Logan village.

The Bell Tree was located in the Strand in Cumnock during the period between the old parish church being demolished and the new one being built. It consisted of a bell hung from an appropriately forked tree (seemingly dead, judging by the picture). The bell was rung daily by bellman and gravedigger Hugh McLelland at 5.30 a.m. and 8 p.m. It was cast by Dutch craftsman Quirinis de Visscher of Rotterdam in 1697, and was said to be 'an excellent casting with a good tone, and ornately decorated with geometric designs and a hunting scene round its border' (John Strawhorn, *History of Cumnock*).

This picture, reproduced from one half of an old stereograph slide, shows an unknown group enjoying the picturesque surroundings of Cubb's Glen on the Lugar Water. Stereographs or stereoscopes were invented in 1838 by Professor Charles Wheatstone (who also invented the telegraph amongst other things), fully one year before Daguerre announced his discovery (the daguerreotype) and Fox Talbot sent papers to the Royal Society giving an account of his new method of obtaining pictures on paper by the action of light (photography). By looking at the slides through a special viewer a 3D effect was obtained. The pictures featured would initially have been drawings, although the development of photography meant that photographic slides such as this one could be produced, with only a select few able to afford to commission private photographs. Cubb's Glen has changed little and remains as popular a beauty spot today as it was in times gone by.

Situated at the top of the Barrhill Road, this beautiful avenue of trees formed the approach to Cumnock Station, and although this has long since closed the trees still stand. The Glasgow, Paisley, Kilmarnock & Ayr Railway Company opened the station on 20 May 1850, having reached Auchinleck two years previously and later extending the line to Dumfries. A second station (Cumnock New) was opened just off Glaisnock Street, where George McTurk Court now stands, in 1872, when the Glasgow & South Western Railway constructed a second line through the town. This necessitated the building of the thirteen-arch Glaisnock Viaduct, the tallest span of which is 75 feet high. It is known locally as the 'Deil's Stone Viaduct' after a large boulder called the Deil Stane, situated nearby. It was believed that if you ran round the stone several times 'Old Nick' himself would appear. The railway withdrew passenger services in 1951 and the line was closed and lifted in 1964, although the viaduct still stands today and is crossed by a public footpath.

Cumnock Station, with the Templand Viaduct spanning the Lugar Water in the background. This was built by Miller & Grainger of Edinburgh and comprises thirteen arches, the tallest being 175 feet high. Miller & Grainger built it only a few years after they completed the Ballochmyle Viaduct across the River Ayr. Its famous 'Big Brig' arch (the tallest masonry arch in the world) is only five feet higher than the Templand Viaduct. Cumnock Station opened up travel opportunities to and from the town, with over 100,000 passengers using it in 1907 alone, but it was closed on 6 December 1965 as a result of the Beeching cuts.

Cronberry Station linked the Ayr to Muirkirk line with the Glasgow to Carlisle main line via Auchinleck, while another service, which opened on 1 July 1870, ran from Cronberry to Annbank before joining up with the Mauchline–Ayr service. The proliferation of railway services in Ayrshire at this time went hand-in-hand with the growth of coal mining and heavy industry, and when mining and other industries began their steady decline in the twentieth century the railways followed suit. Passenger services at Cronberry began being cut in July 1950, and in September 1951 the station was closed to passenger traffic. The line continued handling freight until 1964, but in 1976 closed completely. One story from the station's past tells of a dog which was being transported from Auchinleck to Muirkirk in the guard's van. Upon stopping at the station, the door to the van was accidentally opened and the dog made a bid for freedom, running off up the line and being chased by one of the station porters shouting 'Stop that dog, it's a parcel!' The moorland adjacent to Cronberry, stretching from just outside Cumnock to Muirkirk, is known as Airds Moss and on 20 July 1680 was the site of the infamous battle of the same name. The area has been designated as a Site of Special Scientific Interest and is considered to be one of the most important areas of blanket bog in Britain.

Like many of the small villages that sprung up with the expansion of the mining industry, Cronberry's growth was characterised by the building of miners' rows. Living conditions in these were generally very poor and overcrowded, as recorded in a report by Thomas McKerrell and James Brown in 1913: 'Row 1, there are eighteen houses in this row, and the population is 101', 'there are neither wash-houses nor coalhouses, and the coals are kept under the beds. For this population of 101 there are three closets [toilets]'. 'Row 2, is a replica of Row 1, the population was 113, the open cesspool was in a filthy condition. One of the tenants said to us at this row, "You should have come here in the summer time, it costs us about 1s. a week for flypapers" ' (*Ayrshire Miners' Rows*). Cronberry's football team, Cronberry Eglinton, were founder members of the Ayrshire Junior Football Association in 1889. The league was dominated by Cronberry from the early 1900s to the start of the First World War and 'though no definitive records exist from this time, legend has it that Cronberry were unbeaten at home for ten years between 1904 and 1914 . . . partly due to home fans letting the opposing keeper know what his fate would be if he didn't let in a few goals'! (www.shankly.com). They won the Ayrshire Cup – having actually lost the final – once in their history in 1930 through a successful protest that their opponents had given a false name for one of their players. Cronberry Eglinton was also home for a time, after Glenbuck Cherrypickers, to one of football's most enduring legends, the late, great Bill Shankly.

Cumnock's age of mining is inextricably linked with John Wilson, an ironmaster from Coatbridge who moved into the area in 1843 and took over the old Muirkirk ironworks, which had been established in 1787. Lugar ironworks was opened by his company in 1846 and generated immediate demand for the coal and ironstone that lay below Cumnock. In 1856 the Eglinton Ironworks Co., an Ayrshire subsidiary of William Baird & Co. Ltd., bought out Wilson for the sum of £61,100. The ironworks were then closed down for several years and in 1864 the Eglinton company relocated them to the top of the hill, the new site proving to be more suitable for the furnaces and giving greater opportunity for expansion. In its heyday Lugar ironworks was a huge plant, with five blast furnaces. The Eglinton Co. closed down Lugar ironworks in 1928, Muirkirk ironworks having been closed five years earlier. The site of the works was taken over and used as offices and workshops by the NCB for many years, and is now the location of East Ayrshire Council's local offices.

This picture shows Bello Mill, Lugar, the birthplace on 21 August 1754 of William Murdoch. Murdoch became famous as the inventor of gas lighting and is believed to have carried out many of his early experiments in a cave situated on the banks of the Lugar behind the mill. Before finding fame nationally, Murdoch's family were well-known locally. By 1711 William's father John Murdoch had built a 'wooden horse', a device that could convey him the two miles into Cumnock in a 'very short space of time'. In 1777 Murdoch walked 300 miles from his home at Bello Mill to Birmingham, to seek employment at James Watt and Matthew Boulton's famous Soho Works. Through his employment with the Soho Works in Cornwall, developing the steam engines the company supplied to the tin mining industry, he became the first Briton to construct and use a steam-powered road-going vehicle. By 1795 he had lit his home in Redruth with gas lighting and seven years later the company was using gas lighting outside its Birmingham factory. In 1813 Westminster Bridge was illuminated using gas lighting thanks to the ingenuity of the Lugar man, and in 1817 the Glasgow Gas Light Company was formed.